THE SMELL OF THE KILL

A Play

by

MICHELE LOWE

Dramatic Publishing
Woodstock, Illinois • England • Australia • New Zealand

For my mother, Doris, and my daughter, Isadora.

IMPORTANT BILLING AND CREDIT REQUIREMENTS

All producers of the play *must* give credit to the author(s) of the play in all programs distributed in connection with performances of the play and in all instances in which the title of the play appears for purposes of advertising, publicizing or otherwise exploiting the play and/or a production. The name of the author(s) *must* also appear on a separate line, on which no other name appears, immediately following the title, and *must* appear in size of type not less than fifty percent the size of the title type. Biographical information on the author(s), if included in the playbook, may be used in all programs. *In all programs this notice must appear*:

Produced by special arrangement with
THE DRAMATIC PUBLISHING COMPANY of Woodstock, Illinois

All producers of the play must include the following acknowledgments on the title page of all programs distributed in connection with performances of the play and on all advertising and promotional materials:

"Original Broadway production produced by Elizabeth I. McCann, Nelle Nugent and Milton and Tamar Maltz."

"Special thanks to the Berkshire Theatre Festival, Kate Maguire, Producing Director, for their production in the summer of 2001."

"Originally produced by The Cleveland Play House, Peter Hackett, Artistic Director, Dean R. Gladden, Managing Director.

THE SMELL OF THE KILL

A Full-length Play
For 3 women

CHARACTERS

DEBRA
MOLLY
NICKY

3 OFFSTAGE VOICES (male)

The Smell of the Kill was produced by The Cleveland Play House (Peter Hackett, artistic director; Dean R. Gladden, managing director) in Cleveland, Ohio, in January 1999. It was directed by Scott Kanoff; the set design was by Linda Buchanan; the costume design was by Claudia Stephens; the lighting design was by Richard Winkler; the sound design was by Robin Heath and the stage manager was Dawn Fenton. The cast was as follows:

Nicky	HENNY RUSSELL
Molly	LINDA MARIE LARSON
Debra	BABO HARRISON
Jay	GREG SANDERS
Danny	JOE HICKEY
Marty	DAVID A. TYSON

The Smell of the Kill was produced by Elizabeth I. McCann, Nelle Nugent and Milton & Tamar Maltz on Broadway at the Helen Hayes Theatre, in New York City, on March 7, 2002. It was directed by Christopher Ashley; the set design was by David Gallo; the costume design was by David C. Woolard; the lighting design was by Kenneth Posner; the sound design was by Dan Moses Schreier; the fight director was Rick Sordelet; the production stage manager was David Hyslop; the technical supervisor was Larry Morley; the assistant stage manager was James Mountcastle and the general manager was Roy Gabay. The cast was as follows:

Nicky	LISA EMERY
Molly	JESSICA STONE
Debra	CLAUDIA SHEAR
Jay	MARK LOTITO
Danny/Marty	PATRICK GARNER

THE SMELL OF THE KILL

Lights up on Nicky's kitchen, nine-thirty p.m. There is a skylight above a table and chairs downstage. On the R wall is a door which leads to the dining room and the rest of the house. On the L wall is an arch that leads to the offstage mudroom and bathroom. Above the arch is a clock. There is a center island in the middle of the kitchen.

DEBRA stands at the center island cleaning off plates of half-eaten food while MOLLY and NICKY attend to the dirty kitchen.

DEBRA. Marty shows her the Shaber's house and she says it's not for her. Of course, it's exactly for her. I've met her. You know—lots of makeup, skin like a python. Big chains around her neck. You want to grab her and lock her up to a bicycle rack.

MOLLY. Should I wrap this up?

NICKY. Just leave it on the counter.

DEBRA. Nose job. Breast job. Three-inch nails, four-inch heels—

MOLLY. It's no bother.

NICKY. Just leave it.

DEBRA. Do you know what she calls her husband?

MOLLY. It'll go bad.

NICKY. When it goes bad, we'll wrap it up.

DEBRA. "Butchie."

MOLLY. It'll be too late.

NICKY. So I'll throw it out.

DEBRA. Sounds like a German shepherd.

MOLLY. Then it's a waste.

NICKY. Who cares?

DEBRA. "Butchie"?

NICKY. Who the hell is Butchie?

DEBRA. You haven't heard a word I said.

MOLLY. I was listening.

NICKY. What'd she say?

MOLLY. About a house.

NICKY. Marty sell a house?

DEBRA. I think he's close.

MOLLY. To a couple with a python and a German shepherd.

(NICKY dumps the contents of a large salad bowl into the garbage.)

DEBRA. You're dumping my salad—

NICKY. Nobody ate it.

DEBRA. You could have saved it.

NICKY. It was dressed.

DEBRA. I would have taken it.

NICKY *(holds up a fistful of dripping greens)*. You want it?

DEBRA. That was a really good salad.

(NICKY drops the salad back in the garbage.)

JAY *(offstage)*. Hey, you left a dish out here.

(NICKY opens the door to the dining room and addresses the men.)

NICKY. One dish. One lousy dish. Couldn't one of you get off your ass and bring in one lousy dish? *(A dish comes sailing through the open door, hits the floor and shatters.)* Thank you.

JAY *(offstage)*. You want the ashtray?

DEBRA & NICKY. NO.

JAY *(offstage)*. Because we're starting out here. So whatever you do, stay put.

NICKY. Please don't play in the dining room.

JAY *(offstage)*. We just set up the course.

NICKY. Jay, it's a cup and a golf ball.

DEBRA. Leave them alone.

NICKY. Why can't you play in the living room?

DEBRA. Why can't they play in the dining room?

JAY *(offstage)*. Why can't you all mind your own business?

DANNY *(offstage)*. Molly?

MOLLY. Yes, Danny?

DANNY *(offstage)*. I miss you.

MOLLY. I miss you, too.

DANNY *(offstage)*. Are you still eating?

MOLLY. No, I stopped.

DANNY *(offstage)*. Are you hungry?

MOLLY. No, I'm finished.

DANNY *(offstage)*. You ate beautifully, Molly.

MOLLY. Thank you, sweetheart.

DEBRA. Wait a minute, don't start! Marty? *(No answer.)*
Marty? *(No answer.)*
NICKY. MARTY!
MARTY *(offstage)*. What?
DEBRA. I need my purse.
MARTY *(offstage)*. What for?
DEBRA. My lipstick.
MARTY *(offstage)*. You don't need it.
NICKY. Yeah, you do.
MARTY *(offstage)*. Nobody's looking at you, Debra ...
DEBRA. Nicky is.
NICKY. Let her go. *(She kicks DEBRA out the door.)* Just go.

(DEBRA exits.)

MARTY *(offstage)*. Hurry up.
DEBRA *(offstage)*. Ignore me completely.
JAY *(offstage)*. Watch the cup, watch the ball, watch the
cup, watch the ball ...

(NICKY brings out a bottle of brandy and three glasses.)

NICKY. He stroked my leg.
MOLLY. No.
NICKY. While I was clearing.
MOLLY. He didn't.
NICKY. Like this he did it. *(She strokes MOLLY's leg.)*
MOLLY. No.
NICKY. Yes.
MOLLY. He doesn't mean anything by it.
NICKY. He's going to get himself in trouble some day.
MOLLY. How?

NICKY. I bet he does it to those women he takes around in his car. I bet he does it in the houses. I'm telling you, he does it.

MOLLY. But he's so quiet.

NICKY. Last month at Sarah's, he did the same thing to her.

MOLLY. No.

NICKY. That's why she didn't come tonight.

MOLLY. Because of Marty?

NICKY. Bingo.

MOLLY. He's never touched me.

NICKY. Never?

MOLLY. Not that I know of.

NICKY. He touches me one more time, I'm gonna tell Debra.

MOLLY. You tell Jay?

NICKY. He'd kill him. He doesn't even like Marty.

MOLLY. Neither does Danny. I always thought Jay liked him.

NICKY. Can't stand him.

MOLLY. See what you know about a person.

DEBRA (offstage). Sorry, Jay.

JAY (offstage). She kicked my ball—that's a do-over!

(DEBRA enters.)

DEBRA. Nicky, I can't find my purse.

NICKY. It's in the mudroom.

DEBRA (crosses left). Don't I look like Marty giving a house tour? (And exits to the mudroom.)

NICKY. And he goes to the mall.

MOLLY. Marty?

NICKY. In the afternoons.
MOLLY. No.
NICKY. Instead of showing houses.
MOLLY. You saw him?
NICKY. You can't miss him. He tries to pick up girls in front of the Chess King.
MOLLY. Eew. Debra would die.
NICKY. Die.

(DEBRA enters.)

DEBRA. Nicky, I can't find it.
NICKY. It's probably in the hall closet.
DEBRA. Would you...?
NICKY. Yeah sure. *(She exits to the dining room.)* Coming through!
JAY *(offstage).* Hey! Hey! Hey!
NICKY *(offstage).* I kicked it under the cactus.
JAY *(offstage).* Jesus, Nicky!
DEBRA. Molly?
MOLLY. What?
DEBRA. Has Danny said anything?
MOLLY. About what?
DEBRA. About Jay.
MOLLY. About Jay and what?
DEBRA. About Jay going to jail.
MOLLY. Yes, I heard that.
DEBRA. Terrible.
MOLLY. Awful.
DEBRA. Horrible.
MOLLY. Should we say anything?
DEBRA. Absolutely not.

MOLLY. Are you sure?

DEBRA. Yes. Besides, Marty says that in most of these cases, they get off anyway.

MOLLY. Do you think people know?

DEBRA. We know.

MOLLY. Other than us?

DEBRA. There was a blurb.

MOLLY. When?

DEBRA. Yesterday.

MOLLY. Where?

DEBRA. Tribune.

MOLLY. No.

DEBRA. Less than a blurb. Two sentences, big deal.

MOLLY. Did they mention Nicky?

DEBRA. They don't mention wives until the trial. He's only been indicted. Do you want to see the article? I clipped it.

MOLLY. I couldn't bear it.

DEBRA. Take you two seconds to read.

MOLLY. It's too upsetting.

DEBRA. I'll send you a Xerox.

MOLLY. No, thanks.

DEBRA. I'll put it in the mail, so you have it. You don't have to look at it.

MOLLY. I wonder how she feels.

DEBRA. Well, you can see how she looks.

MOLLY. I think she's brave.

DEBRA. You know why Sarah canceled, don't you? It was Ernie. Ernie said he wouldn't be caught dead in this house.

MOLLY. He didn't.

DEBRA. Do you see them here?

MOLLY. No, I don't.

DEBRA. If Jay had embezzled ten million I wouldn't have been able to come. Thank God it was only seven. Seven is Marty's moral limit.

MOLLY. Will Sarah and Ernie come back?

DEBRA. I don't know.

MOLLY. Are they coming to your house?

DEBRA. When?

MOLLY. Next month.

DEBRA. It's not my turn.

MOLLY. Yes, it is.

DEBRA. No, it's not. I'm after you.

NICKY (offstage). Bad swing.

JAY (offstage). Will you move!

(NICKY enters with DEBRA's purse and drops it in her lap.)

NICKY. Here you go. It was in the hall.

DEBRA. Thanks. (She takes a lipstick out of her bag and applies it.)

MOLLY. Whose turn is it next month, Nicky? I thought it was Debra's.

DEBRA. It's not my turn.

MOLLY. Yes, it is.

NICKY. I think we should skip next month.

MOLLY. Not meet? Can we do that?

NICKY. Why not?

MOLLY. We've never skipped before.

NICKY. Fine, do it at Debra's. But I won't be there.

DEBRA. It's not my turn.

NICKY. Yes, it is.

DEBRA. But if Nicky wants to skip—

NICKY. Nicky wants to.

MARTY *(offstage)*. Debra?

DEBRA. Yes, Marty?

MARTY *(offstage)*. Tell the guys about my round at Winnetka last week.

DEBRA. Marty shot an eighty-seven. *(The guys react.)* He made three eagles on the front nine.

JAY *(offstage)*. What?

MARTY *(offstage)*. *They were birdies.*

DEBRA. What?

MARTY *(offstage)*. They were birdies—she doesn't know what she's talking about.

DEBRA. What did I say?

MARTY *(offstage)*. Never mind.

MOLLY. That's OK, Debra. *(Pours herself a drink.)*

NICKY. Danny said to tell you not to have anything more to drink.

MOLLY. I'm only having one. One is healthy.

DEBRA. You said it gives you nightmares.

MOLLY. It's all right. One little nightmare never hurt anyone.

NICKY. I keep having this horrible dream that I live in Wilmette with a man named Jay.

MOLLY. But you do live in Wilmette with a man named Jay.

NICKY. And we've been married for a hundred and fifty years.

MOLLY. Oh, no, that's different.

DEBRA. My sister's getting married.

NICKY. Which one?

DEBRA. I only have one.

NICKY. I thought you had six.

MOLLY. No, I have six.

DEBRA. He's a doctor. He makes a fortune. She'll never want for anything again in her life.

MOLLY. What kind of doctor?

DEBRA. He's an amputist.

NICKY. A what?

DEBRA. He takes off people's limbs.

NICKY. On purpose?

MOLLY. This girl I grew up with had her left arm removed.

NICKY. Is she OK?

MOLLY. Oh, yeah. She's fine. She plays piano.

NICKY. One-handed?

MOLLY. At the Holiday Inn.

JAY (offstage). Good shot, son of a bitch!

DANNY (offstage). Molly?

MOLLY. Yes, Danny.

DANNY (offstage). I made a good shot.

MOLLY. I'm so proud.

DANNY (offstage). You popped in my head and wham— right in!

MOLLY. Sorry I missed it.

DANNY (offstage). I miss you.

MOLLY. I miss you, too.

DANNY (offstage). Can you see the moon?

MOLLY (looks up through the skylight). Oh, yes.

DEBRA (looks up). Marty says that python woman would kill for a skylight. That's why she won't take the Shaber's house. Frankly, I don't see the appeal.

NICKY. Ten years ago Marty made a big stink out of this one. He called it "God's Little Window."

MOLLY. I think that's sweet.

DEBRA. Ten years ago, I'm sure it was a distinctive selling point.

NICKY. Big selling point. At two o'clock in the afternoon I can cook a chicken on my counter.

MOLLY. Maybe the Shabers could put one in.

DEBRA. No, the Shaber's house is perfect for Butchie and the Python just the way it is. It doesn't need a silly skylight. Skylights are for people who like to look up. These people ... don't.

MOLLY (*still looking up*). Do you really think it is?

NICKY. What?

MOLLY. God's Little Window?

NICKY. Christ, I hope not.

(*A baby cries over the monitor on the kitchen counter.*)

MOLLY. I'll go.

NICKY. No, you stay here.

MOLLY. I don't mind.

NICKY. He'll get too excited if he sees us both. He won't go back to sleep.

MOLLY. I'll stand at the door.

NICKY. I'll be right back. (*She exits.*)

JAY (*offstage*). What are you doing?

NICKY (*offstage*). The baby's crying.

DANNY (*offstage*). It's all right, Jay.

DEBRA. Do you know where Nicky keeps the aspirin?

MOLLY. Are you all right?

DEBRA. Oh, I'm fine. It's not for me.

MARTY (*offstage*). Debra?

DEBRA (*calling out*). Yes, Marty.

MARTY (*offstage*). I've got a headache.

DEBRA. Yes, dear, I'm looking for the aspirin. *(She finds a bottle of aspirin in a cabinet.)* Here they are. *(She takes two aspirin from the bottle and pours a glass of water.)*

MOLLY. Debra, what do you think of Victoria as a name?

DEBRA. Marty had a client named Victoria last year.

MOLLY. Or I was thinking Vanessa.

DEBRA. I like Vanessa. *(She exits with the aspirin and the glass. Offstage:)* Here you go.

MOLLY *(to herself).* Vanessa. Vaneesha. Vaneesha Gilroney. Miss Vanessa Vaneesha Victoria Gilroney. Vanessa, honey, if you're going out you're gonna need a scarf... Vanessa— did you eat all your string beans? You are such a good girl!

(DEBRA enters with the empty glass.)

MOLLY. You know, I think Nicky's baby knows me now when he sees me.

DEBRA. He should. You're over here enough.

MOLLY. She doesn't mind that I come, does she?

DEBRA. She's lucky you do.

MOLLY. She's at work.

DEBRA. I know where she is.

MOLLY. It's hectic for her now between work and the baby.

DEBRA. Poor Nicky. Blah, blah, blah.

MOLLY. She's working on some wonderful new books.

DEBRA. They aren't her books—she only edits them.

MOLLY. I bet she's a good editor.

DEBRA. But, is she a good mother?

MOLLY. Of course she is.

DEBRA. A good mother stays home for the first two years of her child's life. Would you work?

MOLLY. No.

DEBRA. You would be a good mother.

MOLLY. But I'm not working now.

DEBRA. It doesn't matter. A baby needs its mother to be there all the time. The minute I had Billy I stopped working and I never looked back. *(She points upstairs.) You* should have been his mother.

MOLLY. No, no.

DEBRA. Yes, you should have. His mother's never home and his father's going to prison.

NICKY *(from the baby monitor)*. No, he's not.

MOLLY. Debra.

DEBRA. Hello there, Nicky. Didn't realize you could hear us.

NICKY *(from the baby monitor)*. Jay's not going to prison.

MOLLY. Well, that's good news.

NICKY *(from the baby monitor)*. Because I'm going to kill him first.

(DEBRA and MOLLY move away from the monitor.)

DEBRA. I didn't know these things worked both ways.

NICKY *(from the baby monitor)*. Everything works both ways.

MOLLY. We don't really know much about it, Nicky. About Jay.

NICKY *(from the baby monitor)*. How'd you like the article, Debra?

DEBRA. Wasn't much of an article. More like a blurb.

NICKY *(from the baby monitor)*. Molly?

MOLLY. Didn't see it.

NICKY (*from the baby monitor*). I tacked it up in the broom closet, Molly. Take a look. Over by the fridge.

MOLLY. No, that's all right.

NICKY (*from the baby monitor*). Go on.

(*MOLLY opens the closet. There's a piece of newsprint on the inside of the door held in place by a very large carving knife. She glances at the article.*)

MOLLY. I didn't know his middle name was Avery.

NICKY (*from the baby monitor*). Yes, well, now everyone knows.

MOLLY. It's a handsome picture.

NICKY (*from the baby monitor*). The police took it.

MOLLY. I like your Henckels.

DEBRA. Those are good knives.

NICKY (*from the baby monitor*). It was a wedding present.

MOLLY. You use your wedding presents. That's so great.

DEBRA. I still use my wedding china.

MOLLY. Really? I broke most of mine. (*She reaches for the bottle.*)

DEBRA. You shouldn't.

MOLLY. A little bit won't hurt.

DEBRA. You had a little bit.

MOLLY. So I'll have a little bit more.

DEBRA. You got drunk at Sarah's last month...

MOLLY. I didn't...

DEBRA. You fell out of the house when you left.

MOLLY. I tripped.

JAY (*offstage*). Nicky, get out of the way!

(*NICKY enters.*)

NICKY. So, you know about Jay.

DEBRA. Nicky—

NICKY. The police were very considerate.

MOLLY. That's good.

NICKY. They waited until all the neighbors were outside before they took him away.

MOLLY. Nicky, I think you're brave.

NICKY. Why because none of my friends will return my phone calls? Because people are whispering behind my back?

DEBRA. People don't always know what to say in these situations.

NICKY. Sure they do. I've got total strangers coming up to me at the Foodtown all asking me the same question.

MOLLY. Did you know what Jay was doing?

NICKY. That's the one.

DEBRA. People ask you that?

MOLLY. Did you?

DEBRA. Molly—

NICKY. I can't tell you that.

DEBRA. We understand.

NICKY. I'm not trying to be rude—

DEBRA. No, no—

NICKY. The lawyers won't let me talk about it.

DEBRA. Sure, sure. Expensive?

NICKY. The lawyers? Oh, yeah.

DEBRA. Those are the best kind. Marty says if they're expensive, they're good. They'll get Jay off.

MOLLY. Everything will go back to normal soon.

NICKY. No it won't—

MOLLY. Sure it will.

NICKY. I've been making adjustments.

DEBRA. Like what?

NICKY. I've started buying peas.

MOLLY. Peas?

NICKY. Frozen peas. Bags of them.

MOLLY. Do you like peas?

NICKY. No, but they're always on sale.

MOLLY. How much have you bought, Nicky?

NICKY. Twelve bags.

DEBRA. Of just peas?

NICKY. Some peas. Some carrots. I bought nine boxes of string beans. Just in case.

DEBRA. But tonight we had corn.

NICKY. Green Giant.

MOLLY. On sale?

NICKY. Three for a dollar.

MOLLY. Where?

NICKY. The Foodtown.

MOLLY. That's amazing.

NICKY. I can't stop buying cheap frozen food and I'm running out of room.

DEBRA. I'll take some.

NICKY. Don't touch my peas.

DANNY (offstage). Molly?

MOLLY. Yes, Danny.

DANNY (offstage). I love you.

MOLLY. I love you, too. (Pause.) Two weeks ago he forced his way into the ladies locker room at the gym and gave me a dozen tulips.

DEBRA. Sweet man.

MOLLY. Yesterday he bought me seven Gap T-shirts in assorted colors. (Pause.) In the past year he's bought me an I.D. bracelet, an ankle bracelet, and a dog tag with his name on it.

NICKY. Why doesn't he just carve his initials into your arm?

MARTY (*offstage*). Debra!

DEBRA. Yes, Marty?

MARTY. Where are my cigars?

DEBRA. I didn't bring any.

MARTY (*offstage*). You didn't leave them home, did you? (*No response.*) Debra?

DEBRA. I didn't know you wanted them.

MARTY (*offstage*). Debra, what do I always do when I play golf?

DEBRA. Smoke a cigar.

MARTY (*offstage*). So I'll ask you again. Where are my—?

DEBRA. I forgot them.

MARTY (*offstage*). You forgot them?

DEBRA. Yes.

MARTY (*offstage*). You forgot my cigars?

DEBRA. Yes, I did.

NICKY. She forgot them, Marty, let's move on.

DEBRA. I really did forget them.

(*There is the sound of a cat screaming from the living room.*)

NICKY. Jay, what are you doing to the cat?

JAY (*offstage*). I want to see if I can stuff a golf ball up her ass.

NICKY. Jay, let go of her.

JAY (*offstage*). She doesn't mind.

NICKY. Jay, let go of the cat! *(The baby cries over the monitor.)* Jay, put the cat down!

DEBRA. Nicky, that was the baby.

MOLLY. Please let me go up.

NICKY. You won't come down.

MOLLY. Yes, I will.

NICKY. Last time we had to go get you.

MOLLY. I'll come down, I swear.

DEBRA. Let her go.

(MOLLY exits.)

MOLLY *(offstage)*. Excuse me, boys.

DANNY *(offstage)*. Guys, guys, hold it up. *Molly's* coming through!

NICKY. I am a good mother.

DEBRA. I never said you weren't.

NICKY. I like working.

DEBRA. Who's stopping you?

NICKY. My husband.

DEBRA. He's not asking you to stop—

NICKY. He wants me to quit my job so he can use my profit sharing to pay for his lawyers.

DEBRA. Think how hard it must have been for him to ask you to do that.

NICKY. He didn't ask me. He called my secretary and told her to start packing my office.

DEBRA. Couldn't you find another job?

NICKY. This is a really good one, Debra. I've got two assistants. I don't want to leave now.

DEBRA. Can't you bend just a little?

NICKY. No.

DEBRA. I feel sorry for Jay.

NICKY. What about me?

DEBRA. You're fine. Good God, you're made of steel.

NICKY. Oh, you think so.

DEBRA. A month after you gave birth you went back to work.

NICKY. I had a lunch.

DEBRA. You had a baby.

NICKY. I took him with me.

DEBRA. At four weeks! If I had taken Billy out at that age—

NICKY. He would have thanked you.

DEBRA. Maybe this could all be a blessing. If you quit your job, you could spend more time with your son.

NICKY. Your kid's not even home. You put him in military school.

DEBRA. Marty says you can't put a price on a good education.

NICKY. Tell Marty he's wrong. I got your bill for this semester.

DEBRA. I don't know why it went to you.

NICKY. Because I've written the last two checks.

DEBRA. Well, obviously it was an error on the school's part.

NICKY. The bill came from Marty.

DEBRA. Oh. *(Pause.)* You don't think I told him to...

NICKY. No, no, no...

DEBRA. You know, I appreciate what you—

NICKY. But if you need more money...

DEBRA. No, that won't be necessary.

NICKY. I won't be able to loan you any more—

DEBRA. No, no, that's all right—

NICKY. Because they've seized our accounts. *(Beat.)*

DEBRA. What you gave me ... it wasn't part of the money that Jay ... ?

NICKY. No, it was my money.

DEBRA. Oh, good.

NICKY. From my salary.

DEBRA. Wonderful.

NICKY. From the books that I edit that aren't mine.

DANNY *(offstage)*. Molly, what happened?

MOLLY. Nothing.

(MOLLY enters. Her dress is splattered with baby vomit.)

DANNY *(offstage)*. Molly?

DEBRA. What happened to your dress?

MOLLY. It's nothing.

DANNY *(offstage)*. Are you all right?

MOLLY *(shrugging it off)*. I'm fine.

NICKY. The baby upchucked on you, didn't he?

MOLLY. It wasn't his fault.

NICKY. I'm so sorry. Give me your dress—I'll rinse it out.

MOLLY. No, that's all right.

NICKY. I'll rinse it out. I'll put it in the dryer.

MOLLY. It's OK.

DEBRA. Give her your dress. You've got vomit all over you.

MOLLY. No, I couldn't. *(Pause.)* OK. *(She removes her dress. She wears an astonishing red camisole.)*

NICKY. Good Lord!

DEBRA. Molly!

NICKY. Is that you?

MOLLY. It's very—comfortable.

NICKY. Where'd you get that?

MOLLY. It was a gift.

DEBRA. Look at that. Tulips, T-shirts and lingerie.

MOLLY. It wasn't from Danny. *(Beat.)*

DEBRA. Who was it from?

MOLLY. His name is Jacob. I like Jacob.

DEBRA. Who is Jacob?

MOLLY. He's a friend.

NICKY. You have a friend? That kind of friend?

DEBRA. I don't think this is any of our business. And I'm
sure Molly doesn't want to talk about it.

MOLLY. What do you want to know?

NICKY. How'd you meet him?

MOLLY. In an elevator.

NICKY. How come you never said anything before?

MOLLY. You never stripped me before.

NICKY. What is that, a small?

MOLLY. Medium.

NICKY. What do you think I'd be?

MOLLY. You want to try it on?

NICKY. Can I?

MOLLY. Sure.

DEBRA. Molly, I can't believe you.

MOLLY. Oh, you can try it too, Debra.

DEBRA. How could you do this to Danny?

MOLLY. I'm not doing anything to him. And he's not doing anything to me. That's the problem.

NICKY. I figured you two boinked liked bunnies.

MOLLY. That's what everyone thinks.

NICKY. So?

MOLLY. We don't.

NICKY. Since when?

MOLLY. A while.

NICKY. How come?

DEBRA. That's between her and ...

MOLLY. He comes home at midnight five days a week ...

DEBRA. Because he's working ...

MOLLY. On weekends, he sleeps ...

DEBRA. Because he's tired.

MOLLY. He's boring ...

DEBRA. Get a hobby.

MOLLY. I *got* a hobby.

NICKY. So you're having sex with this other guy?

MOLLY. Lots.

DEBRA. Does he know you're married?

MOLLY. Oh, he doesn't mind. He's married too.

DEBRA. What if you got pregnant?

MOLLY. Wouldn't that be great!

NICKY. So you're trying to have a baby with this guy?

MOLLY. You know what his nickname is? Lucky.

DEBRA. Does he know what you're doing?

MOLLY. I don't want to have a baby when I'm fifty, Debra.

DEBRA. Maybe you're not supposed to have a baby.

NICKY. Shut up, Debra.

MOLLY. It's all right. *(To DEBRA.)* I am supposed to. I
know I am. I was pregnant once. You didn't know that.

DEBRA. With who?

MOLLY. With Danny.

NICKY. When was this?

MOLLY. Right after we got married. We were gonna have
a big family. Five kids.

NICKY. Five?

MOLLY. That's what he said.

DEBRA. So what happened?

MOLLY. When I told him I was pregnant, he said he didn't want the noise.

NICKY. The noise?

MOLLY. He didn't want anything interfering.

NICKY. With what?

MOLLY. With us. He liked "us." He wanted it to just be us.

NICKY. And the five kids?

MOLLY. He wanted to wait.

DEBRA. For what?

MOLLY. I've been waiting for twelve years.

DANNY (*offstage*). Molly!

MOLLY. Yes, Danny?

DANNY (*offstage*). Just checking in.

MOLLY. I'm still here.

DANNY (*offstage*). I miss you.

MOLLY. I miss you, too.

(*The door swings open.*)

JAY (*offstage*). What's for dessert?

NICKY. Nothing.

JAY (*offstage*). Make us something.

NICKY. I'll make coffee.

JAY (*offstage*). To go with the coffee.

NICKY. Like what?

JAY (*offstage*). Something chocolate.

MARTY (*offstage*). Debra, what are those cookies I like?

DEBRA. Mallomars.

JAY (*offstage*). Yeah, Mallomars!

NICKY. There are no Mallomars. *(Golf balls roll in under the open door.)* Jay, you're letting in the balls.
DEBRA. Marty—
JAY *(offstage)*. Why didn't you get cake?
NICKY. Jay, shut the door.

(DEBRA and MOLLY try to catch the golf balls.)

JAY *(offstage)*. I'm hungry.
NICKY. You just ate.
JAY *(offstage)*. That was an hour ago.

(The golf balls are coming faster.)

DEBRA. They're coming too fast!
NICKY. Jay, shut the door!
MARTY *(offstage)*. What's the matter, Debra? Too much for you?
DEBRA. Marty, why are you doing this?

(NICKY tries to close the door. JAY fights to keep it open.)

JAY *(offstage)*. Any cheese and crackers left?
NICKY. No.
JAY *(offstage)*. Duck paté?
NICKY. Go fuck yourself, Jay.
JAY *(offstage)*. A couple of chicken legs?
NICKY. Get off the door.
JAY *(offstage)*. What about croutons?
NICKY. Come on, Debra, push...

(DEBRA joins NICKY and together they push.)

MARTY & DANNY (*offstage*). We want croutons!
JAY, MARTY & DANNY (*offstage*). We want croutons!
We want croutons!

(*The door is shut. NICKY locks it. MOLLY carries an armful of golf balls.*)

MOLLY. What should we do with them?
NICKY. Put them in that bowl.

(*MOLLY and DEBRA deposit the golf balls in a bowl in the center of the kitchen table.*)

DEBRA. Why didn't you make dessert?
NICKY. Sarah was supposed to bring it.
DEBRA. I would have made it.
MARTY (*offstage*). Give us back our balls!
NICKY. No.
DEBRA. Make them something to eat.
NICKY. We just ate!
JAY (*offstage*). Nicky, open the door.
NICKY (*to JAY*). Play something else.
JAY (*offstage*). I said open this door!
NICKY. I'm making dessert!

(*The men rejoice. NICKY takes out an electric hand mixer and a container of heavy cream and begins to make whipped cream. MOLLY reaches for the brandy*).

DEBRA. Molly, no more.
MOLLY. It's all right.
DEBRA. What about the bad dreams?

MOLLY. I don't mind. As long as I don't talk in my sleep.

NICKY. My father used to talk in his sleep. He would drink every night until he passed out. Then around three a.m. he'd start yelling.

MOLLY. Yelling at who?

NICKY. My mother and I would wait it out in the kitchen...

MOLLY. Yelling at *you*?

NICKY. Me, my mother, anybody who would listen. Over and over, he just kept screaming for more. "More! MORE!"

DEBRA. More of what?

NICKY. We asked him, he didn't know.

MOLLY. I always dream I'm in water.

NICKY. Floating, swimming—?

MOLLY. Drowning.

DEBRA. I always dream about a house. Last night it was a Frank Gehry on a cliff in San Francisco with 360-degree views of the city, the bay and the bridge—with a Starn Twins diptych over a blue suede sectional in the living room. There were six bedrooms, an exposed plywood library and a pale green, almost like a Bakelite green refrigerator in the kitchen— Oh, you should have seen it. I went through it room by room. And when I was finished...

NICKY. Marty still couldn't sell it.

DEBRA. He could sell your house.

NICKY. It's not for sale.

DEBRA. You'd make a fortune.

NICKY. Jay's making home improvements.

DEBRA. Like what?

NICKY. He bought himself a meat locker.

MOLLY. What for?

NICKY. For his meat.

MOLLY. From the butcher?

NICKY. From the forest. It's hunting season, don'tcha know. So now, when he comes home with bleeding Bambi, he has some place to put him. He goes downstairs, opens his brand new meat locker, and hangs him up.

DEBRA. I've never seen a meat locker in a house.

NICKY. You'll have to get Jay to show it to you. He gives special tours on weekends.

DEBRA. No, thank you.

NICKY. Every Saturday morning he goes down there, kill or no kill, just to take a smell. It gives him a hard-on. Then he comes upstairs and throws me on the bed.

MOLLY. You have deer in your basement?

NICKY. Baby, twenty minutes ago you had deer on your plate.

MOLLY. That was deer?

NICKY. He's having one of the heads stuffed for the dining room.

MOLLY. Stuffed to eat?

NICKY. To hang. Stuffed to hang on the wall.

DEBRA. May I ask, why the dining room?

NICKY. Closer to the flesh.

MOLLY. You made Bambi for dinner?

NICKY. Jay made it. I don't go near his deer.

MOLLY. I'm gonna be sick.

DEBRA. Molly, don't.

MOLLY. I'm gonna throw up. *(She begins to gag.)*

NICKY *(pointing)*. Mudroom.

(MOLLY exits to the mudroom.)

DEBRA. I thought you said you didn't have any money.

NICKY. We don't.

DEBRA. Jay just bought a meat locker. How much did that cost?

NICKY. Ask American Express. *(She finishes the whipped cream, pours it over the golf balls and shoves six spoons into the bowl.)*

DEBRA. What is that?

NICKY. Dessert.

DEBRA. Do we just eat the top?

(NICKY reaches under the sink and pulls out a can of bug spray. She aims it into the whipped cream. DEBRA reaches for the can. She and NICKY struggle for the can until DEBRA gets it away.)

DEBRA. What are you *doing*?

NICKY. I thought I saw a bug.

DEBRA. Jesus. What's the matter with you?

NICKY. My husband went out and spent eight thousand dollars on a meat locker. We don't have that money.

DEBRA. You will when you quit your job.

NICKY. I'm not quitting.

DEBRA. Jay needs you.

NICKY. Jay needs cash.

DEBRA. What difference does it make?

NICKY. Big difference.

DEBRA. How often do you get a chance to do something so grand, so noble for someone?

NICKY. You don't understand—

DEBRA. To save his life! You'd get no joy doing that?

NICKY. None.

DEBRA. He's your husband.

NICKY. For the moment.

DEBRA. You wouldn't leave Jay.

NICKY. No, I *couldn't* leave him.

DEBRA. Good.

NICKY. Because everything we have is in his name.

DEBRA. Well, that was stupid.

NICKY. Yes, it was.

DEBRA. Look, every couple has their problems. They argue. They say awful things. Sometimes they don't see each other for a while—to let things cool down.

NICKY. Is that what you and Marty do?

DEBRA. What?

NICKY. Separate.

DEBRA. When?

NICKY. After you fight.

DEBRA. We don't fight.

NICKY. Oh, come on, Debra.

DEBRA. Why would I fight with Marty?

NICKY. Everybody fights.

DEBRA. I'm not like you. I don't have your—

NICKY. What?

DEBRA. Never mind.

NICKY. What? What do I have?

DEBRA. You're always so—

NICKY. Yeah?

DEBRA. You're very—

NICKY. What?

DEBRA. I hear you sometimes and I watch these things fly right out of your mouth—

NICKY. *You mean spit?*

DEBRA. No, no... I mean sparks.

NICKY. Sparks.

DEBRA. Yes.

NICKY. I speak in sparks.

DEBRA. Yes.

NICKY. Do you?

DEBRA. Have the spark thing?

NICKY. Yeah.

DEBRA. No—no.

NICKY. What do you have?

DEBRA. We're not talking about me.

NICKY. We could talk about you.

DEBRA. We're talking about you and Jay.

NICKY. I'm sick of me and Jay.

DEBRA. You and he could start all over right now.

NICKY. How?

DEBRA. After you quit your job.

NICKY. I'm not quitting my job.

DEBRA. Then if you need money so badly, sell the house.

NICKY. Debra, we had the house appraised. We'd lose our shirts if we sold it now.

DEBRA *(hurt)*. Who appraised it?

NICKY *(caught)*. Some guy in the neighborhood...

DEBRA. Marty would have done that for you...

NICKY. I know...

DEBRA. You could have called...

NICKY. It was a fluke. The guy rang our bell...

DEBRA. Why didn't you call Marty?

NICKY. I told you. We didn't plan it or anything...

DEBRA. Then how do you know he did it right...?

NICKY. It's not that involved...

DEBRA. Sure it is. It is involved. It's a science. And Marty is a genius at it! He's won awards for his appraisals... *(Her cognac goes flying all over NICKY's shirt.)*

NICKY. Easy, Debra!

DEBRA. Sorry.

NICKY. Jesus.

DEBRA. You made a mistake. You should have called Marty.

NICKY. The point is, we're not selling the house.

DEBRA. Well, then you'll have to quit. It doesn't sound like you have a choice.

NICKY. As long as I've got a mouth, I've got a choice. *(She opens the refrigerator door and removes a small bottle of club soda.)*

DEBRA. I didn't mean to do that.

NICKY. Yeah, you did.

DEBRA. It'll come out.

NICKY. It better. *(She removes her shirt. Wearing only her bra, she works on the stain.)*

DEBRA *(embarrassed)*. Aren't you cold?

NICKY. No, actually I'm more comfortable than I've been all night.

DEBRA. I think it's good that we're not getting together next month.

NICKY. You bet.

DEBRA. Not that I ever minded cooking.

NICKY. If you ever cooked, you'd mind.

DEBRA. I cook.

NICKY. Oh, yes, you make that soup.

DEBRA. Cauliflower.

NICKY. Homemade.

DEBRA. From scratch.

NICKY. From a can.

DEBRA. That's a lie.

NICKY. Truth.

DEBRA. I make that soup from scratch!

NICKY. You make that soup from cans!

DEBRA. You're wrong. I made that soup last week, it's one of Marty's favorites.

NICKY. Don't worry, I've never told anyone.

DEBRA. There is nothing to tell.

NICKY. And that lime Jell-O mold of yours?

DEBRA. What about it?

NICKY. You buy it.

DEBRA. That takes me two and a half hours to assemble.

NICKY (cutting her off). You go to Hansen's in Glencoe.

DEBRA. I don't know what you're talking about.

NICKY. That mandarin orange cream cheese slime lime Jell-O mold. I think Hansen's got the recipe from a 1929 *Good Housekeeping*.

DEBRA. That's *my* Jell-O mold.

NICKY. I've seen you leave the store with it.

DEBRA. What do you do—spy on me?

NICKY. Debra, you're not that interesting.

(MOLLY enters wearing a man's hunting jacket splattered with blood.)

MOLLY. I hope you don't mind I borrowed this.

NICKY. What are you wearing?

MOLLY. I found it in the mudroom. What is it? Tie-dyed?

NICKY. It's Jay's.

MOLLY. I like your bra.

NICKY. Thanks.

MOLLY. Neiman's?

NICKY. Saks.

MOLLY. Recently?

NICKY. Maybe a month ago.

MOLLY. Are we all taking off our clothes?

NICKY. Debra threw cognac at me.

DEBRA. I said I was sorry.

MOLLY. Come on, Debra, your turn.

NICKY. Yeah, take off your shirt and stay a while.

DEBRA. No thank you.

NICKY. Debra's upset. I just told her that she doesn't cook.

MOLLY. You told her that?

DEBRA. I cook!

MOLLY (sadly). Oh, Debra. (Baby cries.) I'll go.

NICKY. No, let him cry it out.

MOLLY. I'll just go to the bottom of the stairs.

NICKY. Molly, if he stops crying come back—

(MOLLY exits.)

DEBRA. There's blood all over that jacket.

NICKY. Yes, and for God's sake, don't tell her.

DEBRA. I won't.

NICKY. She'd flip right out.

(MOLLY enters. The baby has stopped crying.)

MOLLY. He stopped.

NICKY. I heard.

MOLLY. The guys aren't out there.

DEBRA. Where'd they go?

MOLLY. Maybe they went for a walk.

NICKY. Yeah. Maybe they're walking off the deer.

DEBRA. It's good Jay has his friends. He needs support right now.

NICKY. Jay needs to rob a bank right now.

DEBRA. If I had the chance to save Marty I wouldn't hesitate for a minute.

NICKY. You mean if he forgot to wipe his ass?

DEBRA. If Marty gave me the opportunity Jay is giving you—

NICKY. Opportunity?

DEBRA. I'd do it gladly.

NICKY. No matter what it cost?

DEBRA. Absolutely.

NICKY. Bullshit.

DEBRA. Truth!

NICKY. If push came to shove—

DEBRA. I'd do anything for Marty.

NICKY. God, Debra, you are so perfect.

DEBRA. No. I'm just not like you. I don't take off my shirt and parade around in my underwear.

NICKY. You should try it.

DEBRA. No thanks.

NICKY. What're you afraid of?

DEBRA. I don't have to prove anything to you.

NICKY. Yeah, you do. (*She moves closer to DEBRA.*)

DEBRA. Go away.

NICKY. Come on, let's see.

DEBRA. Go away, I said.

NICKY. Come on, I'll puke on you and you can take your shirt off. (*She sticks her finger down her throat.*) Uuh.

DEBRA. Oh, Nicky.

MOLLY. Nicky, don't, you're making me queasy.

NICKY. Uuuuh!

(DEBRA moves away. NICKY chases her.)

DEBRA. Come on, Nicky.

MOLLY *(gagging)*. Ugh.

NICKY. UUUGH!

DEBRA. Oh.

MOLLY. Ugh.

NICKY. UUUGH!

DEBRA. Oh.

NICKY. UUUUUHHH!

MOLLY. Ugh.

NICKY. UUUUHHHHH!!!!

DEBRA. Nicky, it's not funny.

NICKY. UUUUUHHH!! Don't be such a priss.

DEBRA. Get away from me.

NICKY. Come on, show me!

DEBRA. I'm not taking my shirt off.

NICKY. Then I will. *(She rips off DEBRA's blouse and reveals a frothy lace bra.)* Holy shit.

MOLLY. Debra?

DEBRA. You ripped my blouse—what's the matter with you?

NICKY. I'll buy you another one.

DEBRA. You can't, you don't have any money. I'm going home.

MOLLY *(stops her)*. No, Debra, wait—wait. It's beautiful. Really, I think you look beautiful.

DEBRA. Really?

MOLLY. I like it.

DEBRA. It's French.

MOLLY. Nicky, doesn't Debra look pretty?

NICKY. Doesn't look French.

DEBRA. I'm leaving. (*Exits to the mudroom.*)

MOLLY. It didn't look French to me, either. (*Beat.*)

NICKY. Was she always like this?

MOLLY. You know her better than me.

NICKY. Didn't you help her with her kitchen?

MOLLY. I helped her pick out her toaster.

NICKY. It's a nice kitchen.

MOLLY. When she finished it, the contractors gave her a plaque.

NICKY. She spent a fortune.

MOLLY. A fortune.

NICKY. Molly?

MOLLY. What?

NICKY. Have you ever been poor?

MOLLY. You mean like Debra?

NICKY. Debra isn't poor. She makes poor choices. She cooks poorly. But she isn't poor.

MOLLY. You mean like that family with the Ford Focus?

NICKY. I mean poor, Molly—really poor.

MOLLY. You mean like those people who take the train to Florida?

NICKY. Worse than that.

MOLLY. I can't imagine.

NICKY. Neither can I.

MOLLY. I come from money.

NICKY. Do you?

MOLLY. Oh, yeah.

NICKY. Money's good.

MOLLY. Money's great.

NICKY. It comes in handy.

MOLLY. It sure does.

NICKY. But it doesn't take the place of—

MOLLY. No, it doesn't. *(Beat.)*

NICKY. Of what?

MOLLY. Babies.

NICKY. Oh. *(Beat.)*

MOLLY. What do you think about Jacob? You think it's wrong?

NICKY. I don't know, Molly.

MOLLY. You think it's a sin?

NICKY. Ask Debra, don't ask me—

MOLLY. You can tell me—

NICKY. What do you care what I think?

MOLLY. Of course I care.

NICKY. Why? The only reason you know me is because our husbands went to college together. We sit in one of our kitchens every month and bullshit, so what? Do you know the name of one book I've ever worked on?

MOLLY. You don't talk about it.

NICKY. You don't ask.

MOLLY. After all this time you want me to ask questions now? Wouldn't that be embarrassing?

NICKY. I don't even know what you do.

MOLLY. I don't do anything.

NICKY. For God's sake, Molly, you're an intelligent woman.

MOLLY. Am I?

NICKY. Yes. You must do something.

MOLLY. I'm raising my children.

NICKY *(gently)*. Molly, you don't have any children.

MOLLY. Then I don't do anything.

(DEBRA enters wearing a man's shirt.)

DEBRA. Thank you for a lovely evening.

NICKY. Don't go away mad.

DEBRA. I'm not mad.

NICKY. Good.

DEBRA. Good night. I'll return the shirt. And by the way, Molly, darling, you've got blood all over you. *(Exits.)*

MOLLY. AHHH!

NICKY. Molly, Molly, it's OK, it's OK. It's old blood. It's nothing. It's OK.

(MOLLY rips off the jacket and throws it down.)

MOLLY. I didn't know what it was.

NICKY. I know.

MOLLY. Did I get any on me?

NICKY. No.

MOLLY. It's disgusting.

NICKY. It is.

MOLLY. I've never heard of anything so gross. How can you live like this?

NICKY. I don't know. He's gone meat crazy. He's got everything down there: quail, duck, part of an elk. *(She exits to the mudroom and returns with sweaters for MOLLY and herself.)*

MOLLY. How can you sleep with a meat locker in your basement?

NICKY. I peeked in there once. He's got some of the animals sitting on the floor, frozen stiff, with their eyes wide open.

MOLLY. I don't want to know.

NICKY. When I met Jay he was a vegetarian. He was a Democrat. He used to bake bread.

MOLLY. Bread?

NICKY. Whenever we got into a fight, he'd make me these little rolls. And then we'd throw them at each other.

MOLLY. That's darling.

NICKY. I hate him.

MOLLY. I know.

NICKY. I mean it—I really hate him.

MOLLY. I hear that.

NICKY. It isn't fair.

MOLLY. It isn't. He made a bad mistake.

NICKY. Then let him pay for it.

(DEBRA enters.)

DEBRA. I can't find the boys.

MOLLY. Are the cars still out there?

DEBRA. Yes.

NICKY. Then they're around.

DEBRA. I'll be in the car.

MOLLY. Come back, Debra.

NICKY. Sit down, Debra.

(The baby cries.)

MOLLY. Oh, I'll go. *(She exits.)*

NICKY. No, Molly, I'll go. He probably needs his diaper changed... *(She exits, then reenters.)* Too late. *(Beat.)*

DEBRA. Did you pay for the appraisal? Marty never charges—his appraisals are all free. Maybe it would be worth it for Marty to do another one—he might have a different idea...

NICKY. We're not selling, Debra.

DEBRA. What number did he give you—the broker who appraised it?

NICKY. I don't remember.

DEBRA. Would you tell me if I was close?

NICKY. I honestly don't—

DEBRA. Just for fun. *(Pause.)* Was it—a million two five? *(Pause.)* Was it?

NICKY. He told you.

DEBRA. No, I swear to God.

NICKY. Then Jay must have told Marty.

DEBRA. No, no, I just took a guess. I used to do this for a living, you know.

NICKY. Well—you were right.

DEBRA. You're not just saying that to make me feel good?

NICKY. Why would I do that?

MOLLY *(from the baby monitor)*. Hello, there, you sweet thing. You are so sweet. Molly had dinner and now she's gonna have you for dessert. Nicky?

NICKY. Yes, Molly?

MOLLY *(from the baby monitor)*. I'm going to sing to him now, OK?

NICKY. Softly.

MOLLY *(singing)*. "Hush little baby don't say a word... Mama's gonna buy you a mockingbird..."

NICKY. My mother stood at the door every night at six o'clock waiting for my father to come home.

MOLLY *(singing)*. "And if that mocking bird don't sing, Mama's gonna buy you a diamond ring..."

NICKY. Dinner on the table, cocktail weenies warming in the oven. Clean apron. She'd be peeking through the curtains sweating. She lived in fear that he wouldn't come home. That one day he'd change his mind and just keep going.

MOLLY (singing). "And if that diamond ring turns brass..."

DEBRA. Where would he go?

MOLLY (singing). "Mama's gonna buy you a looking glass..."

NICKY. I don't know. Maybe someplace they had "more."

MOLLY (whispering). Nicky?

NICKY. Yes, Molly.

MOLLY (whispering). He's asleep.

NICKY. Good work.

MOLLY (whispering). He's a beautiful baby, Nicky.

NICKY. Thank you.

MOLLY (whispering). I love him very much.

NICKY. I'm sure he loves you very much, too. (To DE-BRA.) She's good with him.

DEBRA. You're lucky she comes as much as she does.

NICKY. Yes, I know.

DEBRA. Being a mother is difficult for some women.

NICKY. Is it?

(MOLLY enters.)

NICKY. Nice song.

MOLLY. Thanks. Jacob taught it to me.

DEBRA. He has children?

MOLLY. Oh, yeah. Two sets of twins.

(A loud pounding noise comes from the basement.)

DEBRA. What is that?

NICKY. The guys are probably in the basement.

(Again, there is a tremendous pounding.)

DEBRA. What are they doing?

NICKY. SHUT UP DOWN THERE!

DEBRA. Maybe Jay's showing them the meat locker.

NICKY. Go find out what they want.

DEBRA. Why me? This is your house.

NICKY. Give a house tour of the basement.

DEBRA. I'm not going down there.

NICKY. Molly?

MOLLY. I don't do well in the dark.

NICKY. All right. I'll go. *(She opens the broom closet and yanks the knife out of the newsprint.)* I love the dark. *(She exits.)*

MOLLY. You don't approve of Jacob.

DEBRA. Danny's a wonderful man. Danny would do anything for you.

MOLLY. Except sleep with me.

DEBRA. You still don't go out and find the first—

MOLLY. He wasn't the first.

DEBRA. Oh, Molly— If you and Danny ever separated you'd end up like Mary Beth Frazier living in a one bedroom apartment, begging her friends to fix her up on dates, working for a man half as smart as she is.

MOLLY. She works for Danny.

DEBRA. Oh. Sorry.

MOLLY. I don't want to be her.

DEBRA. Then stay married.

MOLLY. You ever get lonely?

DEBRA. Yes, but I'm not *alone*. I'm not single.

MOLLY. We used to have sex four times a week.

DEBRA. Then something must have happened.

MOLLY. Like what?

DEBRA. You could have done something and not even known it.

MOLLY. How can I know if he doesn't tell me?

DEBRA. They can't tell you—they don't even know it themselves.

MOLLY. They don't know it? Well—darn it. That isn't fair.

DEBRA. No.

MOLLY. That isn't right.

DEBRA. It's just what happens.

MOLLY. And you don't even know what you've done.

DEBRA. No, you don't even have a clue.

(NICKY enters. She opens the kitchen drawers two at a time, searching for something. The pounding starts again.)

DEBRA. What is going on down there?

NICKY. I found them.

DEBRA. Why are they making that noise?

NICKY. They want our attention.

DEBRA. Did you tell Marty I was ready to leave?

NICKY. No.

DEBRA. Why not?

NICKY. He's in the meat locker.

DEBRA. Nicky, could you please go back down there and tell Marty I want to go home.

NICKY. Debra, sit down.

DEBRA. I want to leave.

NICKY. Debra, Marty can't come up.

DEBRA. What do you mean he can't?

NICKY. He can't.

DEBRA. You tell Marty to come out of there this minute!

NICKY. Believe me, if he could he would.

DEBRA. Why can't he then?

NICKY. Because he's locked in.

DEBRA. Oh, my God!

NICKY. This door's been a problem lately.

DEBRA. What about an ax?

NICKY. There is no ax. There's a key.

DEBRA. Where is it?

NICKY. It's in one of these drawers.

MOLLY. Nicky...

DEBRA. When did you see it last?

NICKY. Last week.

DEBRA. Is it there?

NICKY. I don't see it.

DEBRA. Something terrible's going to happen.

MOLLY. Nicky...

NICKY. I know it's in here.

MOLLY. Nicky...

NICKY. It's got to be in here.

MOLLY. Nicky?

NICKY. What?

MOLLY. Are they all in there?

NICKY. All three of them.

MOLLY. Oh, those poor animals. It must be terribly crowded.

DEBRA. Who cares about the animals—they're dead! Maybe
we should call the fire department.

NICKY. No, no, I'll find it.

DEBRA. We shouldn't wait any longer.

NICKY. Debra, nothing's going to happen to the boys.

MOLLY. Is it cold in the meat locker?

NICKY. Yes.

MOLLY. But not that cold, right?

NICKY. Oh, it's cold.

MOLLY. But not *that* cold.

NICKY. It's cold.

MOLLY. How many degrees?

NICKY. Ten.

DEBRA. Oh, my God!

NICKY. Maybe fifteen.

DEBRA. They could freeze in there.

MOLLY. If you couldn't find the key.

DEBRA. They could suffocate in there.

MOLLY. If it wasn't in the drawer.

DEBRA. They could have heart attacks, strokes!

NICKY. Wait a minute—I found something. *(She lifts a key out of the drawer.)*

DEBRA. *They could all die down there!*

NICKY *(the key falls out of her hand)*. Oops.

DEBRA. What was that?

NICKY. Back door key.

DEBRA. Are you sure?

NICKY. Positive.

DEBRA. We can break down the door.

NICKY. It's five inches thick.

DEBRA. We'll tip it over.

NICKY. The thing weighs over a ton. It took three men to bring it in.

MOLLY. I told Danny to wear a sweater tonight.

NICKY. Did he?

MOLLY. No. I said, "Danny, the nights are getting chillier."

DEBRA. Nicky, what does the key look like?

NICKY. How long does it take to make ice?

MOLLY. I don't know—I buy it by the bag.

NICKY. Take a guess.

MOLLY. Let me think.

DEBRA. Nicky, why did you stop looking?

NICKY. What's the rush?

MOLLY. No rush.

NICKY. Jay loves the winter.

MOLLY. Danny loves the fall.

NICKY. If only he knew how to dress for it.

MOLLY. Sit down, Debra.

NICKY. Have a drink, Debra.

DEBRA. I'm going down there.

(DEBRA exits. The alarm on MOLLY's watch beeps.)

MOLLY. Danny bought me a watch with an alarm. He has it set for every two hours.

NICKY. What for?

MOLLY. So I can call him.

NICKY. Why?

MOLLY. He loves me.

(The pounding starts again.)

NICKY. So call him.

MOLLY. He's wearing his beeper. I'm supposed to beep in.

NICKY. What do you say?

MOLLY. I leave little messages.

NICKY. Pick up milk.

MOLLY. I love you.

NICKY. Drop dead.

MOLLY. Stuff like that.

NICKY. I think he'd appreciate a call right now.

MOLLY. You think?

NICKY. Definitely.

MOLLY *(picks up the phone and dials)*. I'd like to leave a message for Daniel Gilroney. Yes, would you tell him that his wife is thinking of him *right now*. Thank you. *(She hangs up.)*

NICKY. Well done.

MOLLY. At night he checks it to make sure the battery's running.

NICKY. Must be aggravating.

MOLLY. Oh, you don't know ...

NICKY. Every two hours ...

MOLLY. No matter where I am.

NICKY. The john?

MOLLY. Oh, sure.

NICKY. Jesus. *(Beat.)*

MOLLY. This is tricky ...

NICKY. Yes.

(NICKY pulls the key out of her pocket. MOLLY takes it and puts it in her purse.)

MOLLY. How cold did you say it was?

NICKY. Fifteen degrees.

MOLLY. Bananas freeze at twenty.

NICKY. Colder than that. *(Beat.)*

MOLLY. Nicky, do you believe in heaven? Where there are angels with wings sitting on clouds listening to Enya? If Danny goes to heaven, he could see our baby. He could explain ... about the waiting.

NICKY. Oh, Molly ...

MOLLY. That it wasn't my fault.
NICKY. No, of course not.
MOLLY. He wouldn't let me give her a name.
NICKY. She was too little, Molly.
MOLLY. I should have done something—
NICKY. You couldn't.
MOLLY. I should have given her a name.

(DEBRA enters.)

DEBRA. What have you done!
NICKY. I didn't do anything.
DEBRA. This is your fault!
NICKY. What did I do?
DEBRA. Isn't there an emergency button in there or something?
NICKY. What for? The dead ducks? So they can buzz us in case they want to come out and make a phone call?
DEBRA. Why haven't you called the police?
MOLLY. Gosh, I didn't think of that.
DEBRA. I'm calling 911. *(She looks for the phone.)* Where's the phone? Where's the phone?

(DEBRA sees the phone on the counter. She lunges for it. NICKY grabs it first.)

NICKY. Grab her!

(MOLLY captures DEBRA.)

DEBRA. OW!
MOLLY. Sorry.

DEBRA. What are you doing?

MOLLY. I'm hurting you.

DEBRA. Stop it!

MOLLY (leans in). Debra, you smell nice.

DEBRA. Get off of me!

MOLLY. But your gray's coming in.

DEBRA. Ow!

NICKY. Let me see.

DEBRA. You're crazy.

(MOLLY jerks DEBRA's head toward NICKY. NICKY
looks at DEBRA's roots.)

NICKY. No, she's right.

DEBRA. Ow!

NICKY. Promise you'll stay still and Molly will let you go.

DEBRA. Let go of me!

MOLLY. She's not going to stay. Let's tie her up.

DEBRA. No.

NICKY. Oh, come on, Debra. (NICKY exits.)

DEBRA (to MOLLY). My arm! You're twisting it!

MOLLY. Sorry.

(The pounding sounds again.)

DEBRA. We have to get them out of there! Listen to them!

(NICKY enters with two pairs of pantyhose.)

NICKY. Will these work?

MOLLY. Donna Karan?

NICKY. Calvin Klein.

(The sound of pounding again.)

DEBRA. Marty!

(NICKY shoves a dishtowel into DEBRA's mouth.)

MOLLY. She's moving, she's moving— Get the chair.
NICKY. Don't let her go.

(MOLLY and NICKY overpower DEBRA.)

MOLLY. Hold her. *(She takes the pantyhose and ties DE-BRA up.)* I've got her.

(NICKY sits on DEBRA and puts her in a headlock.)

NICKY. My brother used to do this to me. *(She looks back at MOLLY tying up DEBRA.)* How'd you learn to do that?
MOLLY. We had boats when I was little.
NICKY. Sailboats?
MOLLY. Yachts.
NICKY. I always wanted a boat.
MOLLY. Boats are fun.
NICKY. Jay didn't want one. He wanted a meat locker.
MOLLY. His mistake.
NICKY. I bet he's thinking that right now—as he watches his penis shrivel up.
MOLLY. It must be teeny tiny by now.
NICKY. I picture them down there right now, desperately trying to keep warm, three homophobic golfers rubbing up against each other. Marty's probably got his hands all over Jay.

MOLLY. Or Danny.

NICKY. Oh, what's the big deal. If it makes them happy, let them! *(MOLLY has finished tying up DEBRA.)* She looks mad.

MOLLY. She just wants attention.

NICKY. Now what?

MOLLY. I don't know.

NICKY. I don't know either. We can't leave her like that.

MOLLY. No.

NICKY. This has got to work for everyone.

MOLLY. Right.

NICKY. Maybe we should vote.

MOLLY. I never vote.

NICKY. Oh, Molly, why not?

MOLLY. I forget to.

NICKY. Ask Debra if she wants to vote.

MOLLY. Debra, if I take out the dishtowel will you scream again? *(DEBRA shakes her head.)* I'm trusting you, Debra. *(MOLLY removes the dishtowel.)*

DEBRA. Vote for what?

NICKY. The boys. We can vote them "IN" or we can vote them "OUT."

DEBRA. You wouldn't just leave them in there?

NICKY. Up to the voters. *(She takes a marker and draws a long line down the refrigerator. She marks the left side "IN" and the right side "OUT.")*

MOLLY. Should we put their names up? That way we don't lose track of who's been voted on.

NICKY. Good idea.

(*NICKY writes the men's names down the left side of the refrigerator. DEBRA drags herself and the chair toward the door to the dining room.*)

NICKY. Where is she going?

MOLLY. She can't get far.

NICKY. Everybody ready?

MOLLY. Everybody's ready.

NICKY. I think each woman should vote for her own husband. The decision of the judges is final and must be unanimous.

MOLLY. Unanimous.

NICKY. After all, if we let one of them go free, he could point a finger.

MOLLY. Oh, yes.

NICKY. If it hadn't frozen off.

DEBRA (*stops in her tracks*). Wait a minute, wait a minute, you're saying if just one of us wants her husband released, they all go free?

NICKY. I think it's the only way. Unless you have a suggestion.

DEBRA. No, no, no, I'm with you. It's the only way.

MOLLY. I agree.

DEBRA. In that case, I'll be good.

NICKY. Promise.

DEBRA. I promise. Now, will you please untie me!

NICKY. Molly, what do you think?

MOLLY. She promised. (*MOLLY releases her.*)

DEBRA. Thank you.

MOLLY. Your wrists are red.

DEBRA. And whose fault is that?

(NICKY takes a bag of frozen peas out of the freezer and gives it to DEBRA.)

NICKY. Here.

(DEBRA puts the peas on her wrists.)

DEBRA. Let's vote.
MOLLY. Let's just do it right. Should we do this by open vote? Should we do it by secret ballot?
NICKY. Oh, I don't know. Debra, what do you think?
DEBRA. Secret ballot? Sure, secret ballot.
MOLLY. I only want to do right by Danny. I want him to feel good about this.
NICKY. All those in favor of secret ballot?

(DEBRA raises her hand.)

MOLLY. You lose.
NICKY. Who wants to go first?
MOLLY. Can I go first?
DEBRA. I'll go first.
NICKY. I think Molly should go first. Two against one.
MOLLY. Should I stand up? Should I sit down?
NICKY. Whatever you want. You're among friends. Right, Debra?
MOLLY. I think I'm going to stand up.
DEBRA. Molly, two weeks ago you and I had lunch at Chez Paul.
MOLLY. Right.
DEBRA. What happened?
MOLLY. I had scallops.

DEBRA. Who showed up?

MOLLY. Danny.

DEBRA. Why?

MOLLY. He loves me.

DEBRA. What did he do?

MOLLY. He held my hand.

DEBRA. Did he say anything?

MOLLY. No. He just held my hand and left.

DEBRA. That's it?

MOLLY. He paid the check.

DEBRA. He surprised you, held your hand, bought you lunch, and you'd leave this man in a freezer?

MOLLY. No matter where I go ...

DEBRA. He adores you!

MOLLY. No matter what I do ...

DEBRA. He worships you!

MOLLY. He finds me.

DEBRA. It's wonderful!

MOLLY. I can't take it.

DEBRA. What more could a woman want than a wonderful, adoring ... ?

MOLLY. Asexual ...

DEBRA. Husband!

MOLLY. I want a baby.

DEBRA. OK. You can have Nicky's baby.

NICKY. What are you talking about?

DEBRA. You don't want him.

MOLLY. Can I?

NICKY. No, you cannot! What's the matter with you?

(The pounding starts again.)

DEBRA. Every woman wants a guy like Danny.

MOLLY. You want him?

DEBRA. No, thank you. My Marty is my Danny.

MOLLY. When I'm in the bathroom at home and I close the door, sometimes I can see Danny peeking through the keyhole.

NICKY. Jesus.

MOLLY. He scares me.

DEBRA. You're his wife!

MOLLY. I don't know if I should be the one to decide.

DEBRA. You're not really sure about this, are you?

NICKY. Yes, she is.

DEBRA. You're not convinced that this is the right thing to do.

MOLLY. I—I wish there was another way—

DEBRA. See!

NICKY. This is the way, Molly—

DEBRA. She doesn't want to do it.

MOLLY. I don't.

NICKY. Molly—

MOLLY. Not like this.

NICKY. MOLLY—

MOLLY. I want it to hurt more.

DEBRA. What?

MOLLY. I want him to get hit by a bus. I want him to fall under a train. I want him to get mowed down by a tractor trailer. I want to watch those eighteen wheels grind him into the pavement like he's a bug—

NICKY. OK, Molly, OK—

MOLLY. And then maybe the truck could back up and roll over him again—

DEBRA. Stop it! Stop it!

MOLLY. This—this is nothing.

DEBRA. I know what she's doing. She wants this other fellow, Joshua.

MOLLY. Jacob.

DEBRA. Whatever!

NICKY. No, I don't think that's it.

DEBRA. She's finished with Danny. Now she's on to the next one.

MOLLY. I'm not on to anyone.

NICKY. Molly?

MOLLY. Yes?

NICKY. I need an "IN "or an "OUT." In?

DEBRA. I object! Leading the witness!

NICKY. All right, I'll rephrase the question: Molly, would you like Danny to remain in the meat locker, the meat locker he entered of his own free will, or would you rather release Danny from his destiny, and in fact, play God?

MOLLY. Oh, I wouldn't want to do that. He's in.

NICKY. Thank you. *(She checks off the "IN" column next to DANNY'S name. The pounding starts again.)* My turn.

DEBRA. We already know your answer.

NICKY. There are a few things I'd like to ...

DEBRA. Let's keep going. Let's just move it along. *(She grabs the marker and makes a check next to JAY's name in the "IN" column.)* Jay's in.

NICKY. I was looking forward to that.

(DEBRA writes a bigger check next to MARTY's name in the "OUT" column.)

DEBRA. Marty's "OUT" and that ends that and I'm calling the fire department.

(DEBRA reaches for the phone. NICKY pulls a small handgun out of a cookie jar and aims it at DEBRA.)

NICKY. No.

MOLLY. Debra, Nicky has a gun!

NICKY. Sit.

MOLLY. Debra, sit down. Nicky's upset.

NICKY. SIT!

MOLLY. It's OK, Debra. Come over here. Come sit next to me. *(DEBRA and MOLLY sit down.)* What do you call that, Nicky?

NICKY. It's a gun.

MOLLY. What kind?

NICKY. A small gun.

MOLLY. Does it work?

NICKY. It works for me.

MOLLY. Debra, it won't be so bad. I bet Marty knows lots of people in heaven.

DEBRA. No!

MOLLY. Aren't your grandparents dead?

DEBRA. NOO!

MOLLY. He'll know them.

(More pounding comes from the basement. DEBRA throws herself down and screams into the floor.)

DEBRA. MMAAARRRTTYYY!

NICKY. Get up, Debra.

MOLLY. I've never held a gun.

NICKY. Molly, it's really easy.

MOLLY. Were you scared the first time?

NICKY. Oh, yeah. Debra!

MOLLY. But you look like a natural.

NICKY. I'm pretty comfortable now.

MOLLY. Could I—?

NICKY. Oh, sure. *(She gives her the gun.)*

DEBRA. MMAAARTTY!

MOLLY. Mind if I ask you something?

NICKY. No.

MOLLY. What do you aim for?

NICKY. I have no idea.

MOLLY. The head?

NICKY. The heart?

MOLLY. I would think the heart.

NICKY. Could be the head.

MOLLY. Debra, are you still with us?

NICKY. She's fine.

MOLLY. I don't think she's breathing. *(She gives the gun back to NICKY and kneels beside DEBRA.)*

DEBRA. MAARTTY!

MOLLY. There we go.

NICKY. Come on, Debra, get off the floor. It hasn't been washed since Tuesday. There's probably deer guts on there.

DEBRA. MAARRTYYY!

MOLLY. Debra, I bet this is the best thing that ever happens in your whole life.

NICKY. Deep down I think Jay wants to die. I think he wants to spare his family the pain, the sorrow, the humiliation of a trial.

MOLLY. I've always believed that when one person dies, another person is born.

NICKY. Everything works both ways.

MOLLY. Doesn't have to be a baby.

NICKY. Could be anybody.

MOLLY. Change is in the air—I can feel it.

NICKY. From now on, I want to come home from work and have a wife standing at the door with a plate of cocktail weenies and a bottle of ice cold Stoli. Then I want to watch her make dinner and watch her clean up while I read the paper and watch TV and scratch my ass and drink my vodka and scream at the top of my lungs...

MOLLY. I want to be the old woman in the shoe.

NICKY. MORE!

MOLLY. I want to be her.

NICKY. MORE!

MOLLY. "There was an old woman who lived in a shoe..."

NICKY. MORE!

MOLLY. Come on, Debra, all together: "She had so many children..."

NICKY. MOOOOORRE!

DEBRA. They'll find out you did this.

NICKY. It was an accident.

MOLLY. A mishap.

NICKY. One chance in a million.

MOLLY. Billion.

NICKY. Trillion.

MOLLY. "She had a billion children..."

DEBRA. I'll tell.

NICKY. No, you won't.

DEBRA. I'll tell them you wanted to kill Jay.

MOLLY. Nicky loves Jay.

NICKY. And they'll wonder why you didn't do anything.

DEBRA. I'll tell them you had a gun.

MOLLY. No, no, it was an accident.

NICKY. We never heard them.

MOLLY. We finished dinner and we went out...

NICKY. For a walk...

MOLLY. And when we got back...

NICKY. We had ice.

(The pounding starts, but weaker this time.)

DEBRA. You said it was up to all of us.

NICKY. I lied. *(Beat.)*

DEBRA. He'll haunt you.

MOLLY. Who?

DEBRA. Jay. He'll haunt you for the rest of your life.

MOLLY. Nicky doesn't believe in ghosts.

DEBRA. She doesn't have to. Every time she looks at her son—

MOLLY. The baby doesn't even look like Jay.

NICKY. Yeah he does.

DEBRA. That's your child's father down there.

MOLLY. He won't remember him.

DEBRA. No, but *she* will.

NICKY *(to MOLLY)*. She's right.

MOLLY. Nicky, it's your turn— *(MOLLY takes JAY's name out of the "IN" column.)*

DEBRA. Some day he'll come to you and ask you about Jay—

MOLLY *(presses the marker into NICKY's hand)*. It's your turn, Nicky—

DEBRA. About how he died.

MOLLY. Tell us what you wanted to say—

DEBRA. What're you going to tell him?

MOLLY. Nicky—

DEBRA. What are you going to tell your own kid?

NICKY. I'll tell him—I'll tell him that Jay loved him very much. I'll tell him that Jay was cut down in his prime— like a young buck shot in the heart. I'll tell him that his daddy did not die alone, he was surrounded by his closest friends. *(Beat.)*

MOLLY. You want to do something with this marker?

NICKY *(takes the marker from MOLLY)*. Yes, I do. But first...I want to thank my husband for the whole gun idea.

DEBRA. You don't need a gun.

NICKY. I have to protect myself.

DEBRA. From what?

NICKY. Crooks.

MOLLY. Have you used it?

NICKY. I'm using it now.

MOLLY. Other than on Debra?

DEBRA. I'm no crook.

NICKY. How do I know?

DEBRA. You've known me twenty years.

NICKY. People change.

DEBRA. I haven't.

NICKY. Even the things that are most familiar can turn on you.

DEBRA. I'm exactly the same.

NICKY. Sometimes I look around this house and I don't recognize any of it.

MOLLY. What do you mean?

NICKY. I've made some marks on it. They're not very big marks. But they help me remember. Whenever I wonder if I'm in the right place, I look for one of these marks. See in there. *(She opens a cabinet door and wiggles her finger through a hole.)*

MOLLY. That hole?

DEBRA. You shot your kitchen?

MOLLY. There's another one.

DEBRA. You wounded your cabinets?

NICKY. So I'd know they were mine.

DEBRA. Couldn't you just put up a sign—"NICKY'S KITCHEN"?

MOLLY. Where else, Nicky?

NICKY. I put a couple in the living room. I had to move some paintings. There's some in the bedroom. Actually, there's one that fit in rather nicely on the headboard. Sometimes I look at things I must have bought at one time or another and I can't remember when or where. They don't look...

MOLLY. Familiar...

NICKY. Riiiight. For instance, that clock. *(She points to the clock above the door.)*

DEBRA. That's been there for years.

NICKY. I can't be sure.

MOLLY. And it doesn't look familiar?

NICKY *(shoots the clock)*. Now it does.

MOLLY *(impressed)*. Now that's a good shot.

(The baby cries.)

NICKY. I'm going upstairs. Molly, you're in charge. *(She gives MOLLY the gun.)*

MOLLY. The head, right?

NICKY. Or the heart. And anything that doesn't look familiar. *(She exits.)*

DEBRA. Does a normal person gun down her kitchen? *(Pause. Whispering.)* Molly, listen to me.

MOLLY. I can barely hear you.

(DEBRA turns off the baby monitor.)

DEBRA. I have an idea.

MOLLY. What?

DEBRA. I know what I can get you for your birthday.

MOLLY. Oh, Debra, you don't have to buy me anything.

DEBRA. Molly, I can help you.

MOLLY. Help me what?

DEBRA. Have a baby.

MOLLY. Debra, I don't think that's possible.

DEBRA. Yes, yes, I can get you a baby. I can get you one.

MOLLY. From where?

DEBRA *(looks skyward).* From upstairs.

MOLLY. Nicky's baby?

DEBRA. Yes.

MOLLY. Oh, you couldn't do that.

DEBRA. Yes, I could.

MOLLY. No, you couldn't.

DEBRA. Yes, I could. You give me the gun. When Nicky comes down, I'll run up and get you the baby.

MOLLY. No, you won't.

DEBRA. Yes, I will.

MOLLY. No, you won't.

DEBRA. Yes, I will.

MOLLY. You'll call the firemen to come.

DEBRA. Molly, I can help you.

MOLLY. Danny wants to buy me a dog.

DEBRA. You don't need a dog, you need a baby.

MOLLY. That's what I said.

DEBRA. Molly, what happens if Nicky comes down and we don't look—*familiar.*

MOLLY. Oh, Nicky knows us.

DEBRA. But what if she *forgets*?

(NICKY enters. She turns the monitor back on.)

NICKY. What'd I miss?

MOLLY. Nicky, who are we?

NICKY. Who are you?

MOLLY. Debra was afraid you might forget us.

NICKY. Don't bet on it.

MOLLY. Is the baby asleep?

NICKY. Yeah.

MOLLY. I've watched him sleep some afternoons. Sometimes he's so still I don't think he's breathing. So I lean over to make sure he's all right, and then I think: what if he's not? What if something terrible's happened and the baby's dead and it's all my fault? I've done it again. I've let another baby die. How could I do that? How could I do the same horrible thing over and over—

NICKY. Molly, Molly—

MOLLY. Nicky, please don't give me the baby. Something could happen. I could do something terrible.

NICKY. Molly! It's OK. The baby's fine.

MOLLY. He's OK?

NICKY. He's OK. Take a breath.

MOLLY. Just don't give me the baby.

NICKY. What is she talking about?

DEBRA *(lying)*. I have no idea.

MOLLY. Yes you do! Debra wanted to trade.

DEBRA. I did not!

MOLLY. She'd get me the baby if I gave her the gun.

NICKY. Molly, give me the gun.

(MOLLY does.)

DEBRA. I never said that!

NICKY. You'd steal my kid!

DEBRA. You'd murder my husband!

NICKY. Not just your husband, mine, too.

DEBRA. Your husband is a common criminal! A thief! An embezzler! At least my husband doesn't ruin his child's life! At least my husband doesn't shame his family!

NICKY. No, but he'll screw anything with two tits and a down payment.

MOLLY. Oh, boy.

DEBRA. How dare you.

NICKY. And you talk about him like he's Gandhi.

MOLLY. Gandhi.

NICKY. "Marty said" this and "Marty said" that—you haven't had an original thought in years. And what kills me is, we thought you were the one with the big brain. You were a double major.

MOLLY. Her?

NICKY. Second in your class…

MOLLY. Her?

NICKY. Phi Beta Kappa.

MOLLY *(to DEBRA)*. What happened to you?

NICKY. I bet he's been fooling around on you for years.

DEBRA. You think I'm so stupid.

NICKY. I don't know. Are you?

DEBRA. My husband sleeps with one woman! ONE!

NICKY. Who's he sleeping with? *(Beat.)*

DEBRA. You know.

NICKY. Say it.

DEBRA. With her.

MOLLY. Who?

DEBRA. The Python.

NICKY. I knew it!

DEBRA. I knew he looked at women.

MOLLY. It happens, Debra.

NICKY. I bet it happens plenty.

MOLLY. Yeah, look at me.

DEBRA. Well, at least he never went for one of you.

NICKY *(lying)*. Never.

MOLLY *(lying)*. Not ever.

DEBRA. I've known about Diane for a while.

NICKY. Who's Diane?

MOLLY. The Python.

DEBRA. He told me everything. Well, actually she told me.

NICKY. You spoke to her?

DEBRA. She called. We talked. She finally found a house she likes.

NICKY. Who cares?

DEBRA. It's my house.

MOLLY. No.

DEBRA. She wants it for her and Marty.

NICKY. You're not going to give her your house.

DEBRA. It's too late. I'm out.

MOLLY. Out where?

DEBRA. Out of the house. They get the house.

MOLLY. Your beautiful house.

DEBRA. I love my house.

NICKY. What do you get?

DEBRA. I get Billy.

NICKY. That's it?

DEBRA. I love Billy.

MOLLY. I like Billy.

DEBRA. Well, you can't have him.

NICKY. That's all you're getting?

DEBRA. I get full custody of Billy. And Marty'll pay for the lawyers.

NICKY. Where'd he get money all of a sudden?

DEBRA. She has money. I made the deal with her. Marty's got no head for business. When we worked together, he'd charm the wife while I'd haggle with the husband. We'd sell one house after the next—bam, bam, bam. We were great.

MOLLY. So what happened?

DEBRA. I had Billy.

NICKY. You stopped working.

DEBRA. I wanted to go back to work but Marty kept putting me off.

NICKY. Why?

DEBRA. Why.

MOLLY. So you waited.

DEBRA. I thought he'd change his mind.

MOLLY. You didn't have a clue.

DEBRA. No.

MOLLY. At least you had Billy.

DEBRA. Billy hates me.

NICKY. Billy doesn't hate you.

MOLLY. If my mother sent me to military school, I'd hate her.

DEBRA. Marty thinks—

NICKY. Oh, for chrissakes, Debra, nobody *cares* what Marty thinks. What do *you* think? *(Beat.)*

DEBRA. I think...

NICKY. *What?*

DEBRA. I think military school is hard on a mother.

MOLLY. It must be very hard.

NICKY. And...

DEBRA. I miss my son.

MOLLY. Of course you do.

DEBRA. I miss my son and he hates me. *I'm* the shitty mother.

MOLLY. Every mother gets to be a shitty mother sometimes.

DEBRA. You don't know.

MOLLY. Every—

DEBRA *(cutting her off)*. You don't. You want to be a mother so badly? Billy hates my guts because I won't let him come home and I won't let him come home because his father doesn't want him around. But Billy doesn't know that. I cover for Marty and I end up being loved by nobody—not my son, not my husband—not my friends...

MOLLY. We love you, Debra.

NICKY. We'd love you more if you kept Marty in the meat locker.

DEBRA. Look, no matter how I feel about Marty I still couldn't—

NICKY. Do you still like Marty, Debra?

DEBRA. Do I like him?

MOLLY. Is he a good person?

DEBRA. There's a lot of good things about him.

NICKY. Like what?

DEBRA. I'm sure there's one thing.

NICKY. Name it.

DEBRA. All right.

NICKY. Go on.

DEBRA. I'm thinking.

MOLLY. Oh, I can think of something.

DEBRA. What?

MOLLY. He weeds the garden in the springtime.

DEBRA *(delighted)*. Does he?

MOLLY. I passed him last year in the car.

NICKY. OK, he weeds.

DEBRA. I never saw him do that.

NICKY. Name something redeeming about your husband other than that he's a weeder.

DEBRA. He opens the door for me when we go into restaurants.

MOLLY. He's a gentleman.

DEBRA. Always.

NICKY. Always?

DEBRA. Always a gentleman.

NICKY. He stroked my leg during dinner.

MOLLY. Oh, boy.

DEBRA. I don't believe you.

NICKY. I swear.

DEBRA. You just want to upset me.

MOLLY. He did, Debra. He stroked her.

DEBRA. Maybe he thought it was my leg.

NICKY. You weren't anywhere near him. *(Beat.)*

DEBRA. You really loved telling me that, didn't you?

MOLLY. No, Debra. She loved telling *me*, but she really didn't want to tell you. *(Beat.)*

DEBRA. You know what's happening down there right now? *(NICKY and MOLLY nod.)* And you have no qualms about walking away?

(NICKY and MOLLY shake their heads.)

NICKY. If the situation was reversed, if we were down there right now, what would Marty do?

DEBRA. Would he let me freeze? Probably. So what does that prove? If we leave them in there, then we're as bad as they are.

MOLLY. I have no problem with that.

(NICKY gives DEBRA the phone.)

NICKY. You want to call 911?

MOLLY. Nicky.

NICKY *(to DEBRA)*. You want the weeder out—call.

MOLLY. We can do this, Debra...

DEBRA. I'm trying—

MOLLY. Try harder.

NICKY. But don't do it for Billy.

MOLLY. Do it for me.

DEBRA. You'll go off with what'shisname and you'll go back to work.

NICKY. So?

DEBRA. What'll I do?

NICKY. What are you doing now?

DEBRA. I'm going to get left behind.

NICKY. How can you get left behind? We're about to kill our husbands. I'm either going to be your best fucking friend for the rest of your life or I'm going to have to kill you, too. *(Pause.)* Molly, forget it. She's not gonna do it. I'm calling the police.

(NICKY reaches for the phone. DEBRA holds onto it.)

DEBRA. No, don't— *(Pause.)* People make mistakes, but do you murder them? Marty's—*awful*—but should I kill him? I don't know, I don't know— He's leaving me for another woman—should he die for that? He's throwing me out of my house—I spent ten years on that kitchen. Billy hates me because of him— But if Marty freezes to death *will I rot in hell?* *(Pause.)* Do I care? *(Pause.)* I don't know. I don't know.

NICKY. Let me tell you what I see: I see a woman staying in her beautiful house—

MOLLY. Baking pies in her gorgeous oven—

NICKY. With her only son beside her—

MOLLY. Home from military school—

NICKY. Home for good.

MOLLY. And never going back.

NICKY. She seems so happy.

MOLLY. Doesn't she?

NICKY. The only mind she has to read is her own. The only person she has to take care of is herself.

MOLLY. And her son.

NICKY. But wait a minute—someone's at the front door.

MOLLY *(knocks on the counter)*. Who's that?

NICKY. It's—the mail carrier.

MOLLY. What could he be bringing them?

NICKY. It's a big fat check.

MOLLY. From a life insurance policy.

NICKY. The woman and her son join hands and dance around the living room—

MOLLY. While a deranged woman with skin like a python bangs on the window trying to get in.

NICKY. The police come and take the deranged woman away.

MOLLY. I've never seen such joy—

NICKY. On any two faces.

MOLLY. That woman with her son—

NICKY. She looks so familiar—

MOLLY. Doesn't she?

NICKY. I can almost make her out—

MOLLY. Yes, she's—she's coming into focus—

NICKY. That woman—

MOLLY. That woman—

NICKY. That woman—

DEBRA. *Is me.*

(DEBRA hands the phone back to NICKY. There is a triumphant group hug and smiles all around.)

NICKY. Bravo, Debra.

MOLLY. We're a team now. I've never been on a team. I almost made the volleyball team but I got cut. And then there was the debate team but I didn't make that either. I tried out for cheerleading in sixth grade, seventh grade, eighth grade—

NICKY. You made the team, Molly.

MOLLY. I know. I'm so excited I could eat a horse. *(She takes a bag from the cabinet and begins to eat. Except*

for the sound of MOLLY chewing, it is strangely quiet.
Long beat.)

NICKY. Listen.

MOLLY. What?

NICKY. They've stopped banging.

MOLLY. They're probably ice cream by now.

NICKY. Vanilla, chocolate, and Rocky Road.

MOLLY *(offers the bag to NICKY)*. Crouton?

NICKY. No, thanks.

MOLLY *(offering her bag)*. Debra?

(No response. DEBRA looks like she's in a trance.)

NICKY. Debra?

MOLLY. Is she all right?

NICKY. Debra!

MOLLY. Debraaaa!

DEBRA. They couldn't thaw, could they?

MOLLY. Gee, I don't know.

DEBRA. It'd be a shame if they thawed.

MOLLY. Well, figure it takes two days to thaw a twenty-two-pound turkey.

NICKY. Yes, but the turkey is already dead.

MOLLY. Right.

DEBRA. What if they just slow down and don't fully freeze?

NICKY. What do you mean?

DEBRA. What if they just congeal?

MOLLY. You mean like Jell-O?

DEBRA. What if they freeze while clutching so tightly to each other, we can't separate them?

MOLLY. What if they stick to the deer?

NICKY. He's got rabbits in there, too.

MOLLY. What if they can't scrape the deer off of them?

DEBRA. They could freeze with deer and rabbit attachments.

MOLLY. If they do freeze as a solid mass, I have no problem burying them in the same pit.

NICKY. Grave.

MOLLY. Grave.

DEBRA. We could have them cremated.

NICKY. There you go.

MOLLY. You know, I'm looking forward to spending a lot more time with you girls. Every month we used to say the same things over and over and now—now we'll have so much more to talk about.

NICKY. We're not going to skip next month, are we?

MOLLY. Oh, we can't.

DEBRA. We can meet at my house—

MOLLY. Or my house—

NICKY. Let's not meet here.

DEBRA & MOLLY. No.

NICKY (to DEBRA). Want to sell a house?

DEBRA. Me?

NICKY. I can't live here.

DEBRA. No, no, you need someone better than me—

NICKY. I want cash.

DEBRA. I can get you cash.

NICKY. No mortgage.

DEBRA. I can get you cash, no mortgage and a bidding war.

NICKY. Deal.

DEBRA. I'll send over the contracts in the morning.

MOLLY. You're not going to move too far away are you, Nicky?

NICKY. We're all going downtown to buy me a loft. Or maybe an apartment on the sixty-eighth floor of something. Then we can put on cocktail dresses and ride the ferris wheel at Navy Pier.

DEBRA. Remember what happened to Sarah's mother when Sarah's father died?

MOLLY. No.

DEBRA. She used to work in that store in Plaza de Lago...

NICKY. No makeup, gray hair, baggy dresses—she was a drudge. Then her husband dropped dead.

DEBRA. Have you seen her recently?

NICKY. She's gorgeous.

DEBRA. She's dating.

NICKY. She's taking dancing lessons.

DEBRA. She's taking Spanish.

NICKY. She's been to Europe.

MOLLY. I could go to Italy.

DEBRA. I've always wanted to pick out my own car.

NICKY. Jay never wanted to take ballroom dancing...

DEBRA. Take horseback riding.

MOLLY. I could go to France.

NICKY. French lessons.

DEBRA. I could learn to paint.

MOLLY. Or sing...

NICKY. Or sail...

(As the kitchen lights fade the women slowly step forward into three pools of light and address their unseen interrogators.)

DEBRA. I don't know what happened.

MOLLY. We went to Jay and Nicky's house. We had dinner.

NICKY. We had deer.

MOLLY (*cheerfully*). I love deer.

DEBRA. Then the men stayed in the dining room to play...

MOLLY. Golf.

NICKY. It's what they usually do.

DEBRA. I've always wanted to learn.

NICKY. He bought the meat locker about a month ago. I was so excited...

MOLLY. Well, I knew he was a hunter...

DEBRA. I have a terrific recipe for rabbit...

NICKY. After dinner we took a walk...

MOLLY. To get ice cream.

DEBRA. Vanilla—

NICKY. Chocolate—

MOLLY. And Rocky Road.

DEBRA & NICKY. Baskin Robbins.

MOLLY. No, just the girls went.

DEBRA. Nicky and I have always been close.

NICKY. Debra's like a sister to me.

MOLLY. My husband and I had a very special bond...

NICKY (*tearfully*). My husband was distraught, guilt ridden, depressed over the indictment. He felt terrible about how it would affect us. I wanted to quit my job to help him, but he said no—he'd figure something out...

DEBRA. Marty wanted me to go back to work, but I enjoyed being home, waiting for him. Dinner on the table, cocktail franks warming in the oven. Clean apron on—

MOLLY. I used to call Danny twenty times a day—just to hear his voice.

DEBRA. Marty worked so hard.

NICKY. We couldn't have been gone more than thirty min-
    utes...
DEBRA & MOLLY. Half an hour.
DEBRA. And when we came back...
NICKY & MOLLY. Gone...
DEBRA. Missing...
MOLLY. Who knows where?
NICKY. Too much to drink...
DEBRA. Too much alcohol...
MOLLY. One minute they're having a good time, the next
    minute—
NICKY. Wham.
DEBRA. The door must have closed.
NICKY. It's been a problem since day one.
MOLLY. And that's what happened, Officer.

(They collectively sigh.)

DEBRA. Do you mind if I call my son?
MOLLY. Do you have any soda?
NICKY. Do you believe in heaven?
DEBRA. They were angels, all of them.
MOLLY. And now they're on their way.
NICKY. Together.
MOLLY. Best friends.
DEBRA. Like us.
ALL. Forever.

(Blackout.)

THE END

DIRECTOR'S NOTES

DIRECTOR'S NOTES

DIRECTOR'S NOTES